Nicolaus Copernicus

Father of Modern Astronomy

Scott Ingram

BLACKBIRCH™
PRESS

THOMSON

© 2004 by Blackbirch Press™. Blackbirch Press™ is an imprint of The Gale Group, Inc.,
a division of Thomson Learning, Inc.

Blackbirch Press™ and Thomson Learning™ are trademarks used herein under license.

For more information, contact
The Gale Group, Inc.
27500 Drake Rd.
Farmington Hills, MI 48331-3535
Or you can visit our Internet site at http://www.gale.com

Photo Credits: cover © Hulton|Archive by Getty Images; page 5 © Giraudon/Art Resource,
NY; pages 7, 35 © Victoria & Albert Museum, London/Art Resource, NY; pages 8, 10, 11,
14–15, 19, 22, 26, 29, 30, 42, 47, 58 © Erich Lessing/Art Resource, NY; pages 13, 17, 51 ©
Archivo Iconografico, S.A./CORBIS; page 18 © Corel Corporation; page 21 © Réunion des
Musées Nationaux/Art Resource, NY; pages 25, 44, 54 © Mary Evans Picture Library; page
27 © Image Select/Art Resource, NY; page 31 © Scala/Art Resource, NY; pages 32, 57 ©
Library of Congress; page 36 © Araldo de Lucas/CORBIS; pages 38, 48 © Blackbirch
Archive; page 39 © PhotoDisc; page 41 © Roger Ressmeyer/CORBIS; page 45 © The Art
Archive/Palatine Library Parma/Dagli Orti; page 52 © Paul Amasy/CORBIS;

LIBRARY OF CONGRESS CATALOGING-IN-PUBLICATION DATA

Ingram, Scott.
 Nicolaus Copernicus / by Scott Ingram.
  p. cm. — (Giants of science series)
Summary: Discusses the youth, education, scientific observations, conflict with religious
teachings and the Church, and legacy of Nicolaus Copernicus.
Includes bibliographical references and index.
 ISBN 1-56711-489-X (hardback : alk. paper)
 1. Copernicus, Nicolaus, 1473–1543—Juvenile literature. 2. Astronomers—Poland—
Biography—Juvenile literature. [1. Copernicus, Nicolaus, 1473–1543. 2. Astronomers. 3.
Scientists.] I. Title. II. Series: Giants of science.

 QB36.C8I54 2004
 520'.92—dc22

                                                            2003016229

Printed in the United States
10 9 8 7 6 5 4 3 2 1

CONTENTS

"At the Middle of All Things Lies the Sun"

By the spring of 1543, Nicolaus Copernicus had been observing the skies over Frombork, Poland, for more than thirty years. A famous mathematician and teacher, the seventy-year-old Copernicus had lived much of his adult life in the city on the Baltic Sea where he worked as an administrator for the church. That work, however, occupied only his days. It was his nighttime observations and calculations of the movements of the heavenly bodies that truly occupied his thoughts.

Now, in late May, Copernicus lay near death, his mind and body incapacitated by a series of strokes. At his bedside was Georg Rhäticus, a young mathematics professor from Nürnberg, Germany, who had been an assistant to Copernicus for several years. Two years before, Copernicus had entrusted his life's work to Rhäticus for publication.

Copernicus's writings, entitled *On the Revolution of the Celestial Orbs*, contain his observations and calculations of celestial movement and refute religious and scientific belief that had been widely accepted for more than one thousand years. Copernicus's theory shattered the age-old belief that Earth was the center of the solar system, with the Sun, Moon, and other visible celestial bodies revolving around it. Instead, Copernicus had concluded that Earth was a planet that revolved around the Sun. The only body that revolved around Earth, he believed, was the Moon. The Copernican theory, as it would come to be known, was so revolutionary that he had shared it only with trusted friends in the twenty years since he had finished it.

Copernicus believed the Earth was not the center of the universe and proved his theory using careful observation and mathematical calculations.

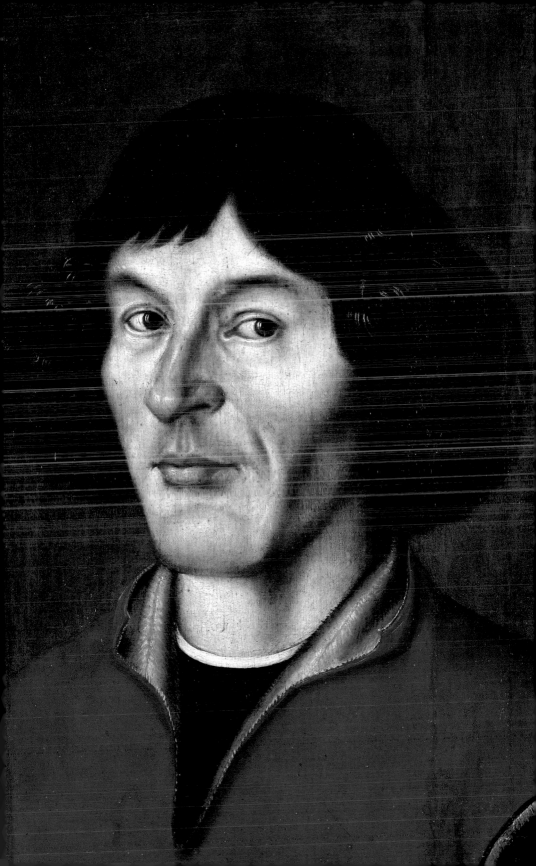

A Difficult Decision

The decision to finally publish the work had not been an easy one for Copernicus to make. In fact, he had considered withholding his work until after his death. The arrival in Frombork of the twenty-five-year old Rhäticus in 1539, however, had changed Copernicus's mind. The younger man had heard rumors that this church administrator in Poland had proved that Earth was not the center of the solar system. Eager to learn more, he closely reviewed and checked all of the older man's work until he had no doubt about the Copernican theory. He enthusiastically offered to take on the task of finding financial backers to pay for the costs of publishing the six volumes that comprised *On the Revolution of the Celestial Orbs.*

Rhäticus wrote in 1541 that after much persuasion, Copernicus had "finally overcome his prolonged reluctance to release his volume for publication."[1] For the next two years, Rhäticus carried manuscript pages of Copernicus's work between Frombork and Nürnberg, Germany, where it was printed.

Finally, in late 1543, as Copernicus lay dying, Rhäticus handed him a copy of the printed work. Copernicus died before he could read it, but to the end, he remained as certain of the theory as he had been when he first stated it many years earlier: "At the middle of all things lies the sun."[2]

A Centuries-Old Idea

Although Copernicus is usually remembered as the first person to suggest that the planets revolve around the sun, others proposed the idea—known as the heliocentric theory—long before he did. The Greek philosopher Aristarchus suggested the theory as early as the third century B.C. The idea, however, ran counter to the beliefs of Aristotle, a more well-known philosopher who claimed that Earth was the center of the universe. Aristarchus's ideas were rejected in favor of Aristotle's, and the heliocentric theory was almost forgotten for fifteen hundred years. Copernicus's name is linked with the heliocentric theory because he was the first to prove it scientifically.

Copernicus's other main contribution to modern science was his reliance upon facts to prove a hypothesis and to duplicate the

The theory that Earth, and all the other planets, revolve around the Sun existed long before Copernicus proved it scientifically.

results of his work. This systematic practice became known as the scientific method. Copernicus's combination of observation, record keeping, and calculations made him one of the first men of his time to follow rigorous scientific procedures and established him as one of the great minds of science. The work over which he labored for most of his lifetime was to formulate mathematical proof of the heliocentric theory.

Copernicus's ideas, however, contradicted the beliefs of the church, which was not only a powerful religious force, but also the most influential social and political power in Europe. For centuries, church leaders and religious followers had based their understanding of the positions of Earth, the Sun, and other celestial bodies on passages from the Bible, which states that the heavenly bodies revolve around Earth.

Ptolemy, a second-century Greek scientist, believed the Sun, Moon, and planets all revolved around Earth. His calculations supported this geocentric theory.

Ptolemy's Studies

A Greek scientist and mathematician named Ptolemy, who studied the heavens during the second century A.D., agreed with the Bible. His calculations of the movements of the Sun, the Moon, and the planets placed Earth at the center of their orbits. This came to be known as the geocentric theory.

By the time Copernicus was born, astrologers saw the universe as a relatively small place with Earth at its center. The movements of the planets and events in the heavens such as shooting stars or the passing of a comet were thought to be divinely created for the benefit of humanity. In sixteenth-century Europe, those who challenged this view were considered heretics who not only ignored accepted scientific fact but disregarded religious principles as well. Given the power of the church, anybody suspected of holding such opinions could suffer severe punishment.

As he made his astronomical discoveries, Copernicus assumed—correctly—that there would be many who thought the accepted beliefs were irrefutable. In fact, while his calculations were widely admired by fellow mathematicians, his conclusion that the planets revolved around the sun was almost totally discredited. Nevertheless, Copernicus's book was widely discussed among astronomers after his death, and admiration for him grew as his colleagues broke down thirty years of work into detail and examined each step Copernicus had taken to arrive at his conclusions. It was through this close examination that Copernicus's work made its greatest contribution. In effect, it changed the nature of astronomy.

Childhood in Eastern Poland

The man who would challenge one thousand years of beliefs about astronomy and Earth's place in the universe was born in the city of Toruń in Royal Prussia, a province of Poland, on February 19, 1473. The youngest of four children, Copernicus was given the name Mikolaj Kopernik, which was also his father's name. The senior Kopernik married Barbara Waczenrode, who came from a wealthy family from Toruń, in about 1463. Kopernik owned a business that traded in copper, and he

Copernicus's uncle, whose room is pictured above, was a high-ranking church official. After Copernicus's parents died, he became the boy's guardian.

participated in local politics. The family was wealthy enough to have a summer residence with vineyards outside of town.

The stable family life and relative wealth was short-lived, however, for the Kopernik children. By the time young Micolaj was ten years old, both his parents had died. From that time on, Barbara's brother, Lucas Waczenrode, became the children's guardian. Waczenrode could afford to take the family under his care because, as the bishop of Toruń, he was a high-ranking official in the church. During the ensuing years, in addition to paying for their living expenses, he provided for the education of the boys, Andrej and Micolaj. Eventually, one of Micolaj's sisters, Barbara, became a nun and his other sister, Katherine, married a Toruń businessman and city official.

Under the guidance of their uncle, Micolaj and his brother continued their education in Toruń until they were both fifteen. In 1488, Waczenrode sent Micolaj to the secondary school at Wloclawek, Poland, where he received the standard education of the time. Micolaj studied Latin and devoted many hours to religious studies.

Fifteenth-Century Education

After three years at Wloclawek, Kopernik continued his studies at Poland's University of Krakow. By this time, his uncle had been appointed bishop of Ermeland, one of the most powerful bishoprics in western Poland. Not surprisingly, Waczenrode recommended that his nephew concentrate on subjects that would prepare him for a career with the church.

Kopernik was deeply grateful to his uncle and did not object to pursuing such a position, but his education at Krakow became much more than an upper-level version of the religious studies he had undertaken in secondary school. His university education, he later wrote, was a vital factor in all that he went on to achieve. It

At the University of Krakow, Copernicus became interested in astronomy and used instruments like the one pictured here.

was during this period of his life that Kopernik began to use the Latin spelling of his name, Copernicus, by which he is known.

During his four years at Krakow, Copernicus studied geography, mathematics, philosophy, and astronomy. Astronomical observation had to be accomplished solely with the naked eye—Copernicus lived more than one hundred years before the first telescope was invented. Nonetheless, he was fascinated by the subject of astronomy.

At that time, astronomy was actually a small part of the so-called science of astrology. In fact, "astrology" and "astronomy" were often used interchangeably. The main reason astronomers observed the movement of celestial bodies was to predict future events. Rulers often consulted astrologers to learn whether the sun and the planets would be in proper alignment for a certain event at a certain date. They might attack an enemy, for example, if the date was favorable for battle. Leaders of the church also regularly consulted astrologers about the future.

The Geocentric Theory

Mastery of astronomy's mathematical equations was necessary for students to understand the calendar, to calculate the dates of holy days into the future, and to use astrology to chart the horoscopes of people from the exact time of their birth. As a student, Copernicus excelled in both mathematics and astronomy. The most widely accepted theory of astronomy during Copernicus's college years was a creation myth that had supposedly been proven by an astronomer named Ptolemy.

Almost all ancient civilizations had stories about the creation of the world, and the vast majority of them placed Earth at the center of the universe. These myths were fashioned thousands of years before the telescope was invented, as were ideas about what the planets were. The word *planet*, from the Greek word for "wanderer," was applied to the seven visible celestial bodies that changed position with respect to the stars. The bodies known as planets to the ancient world were Mercury, Venus, Mars, Jupiter, Saturn, the Moon, and the Sun.

The ancient ideas about planets were expanded upon in the second century A.D. by Ptolemy, who created mathematical formulas that explained and predicted the motion of celestial bodies around Earth. Ptolemy's thirteen-volume work, *Almagest*

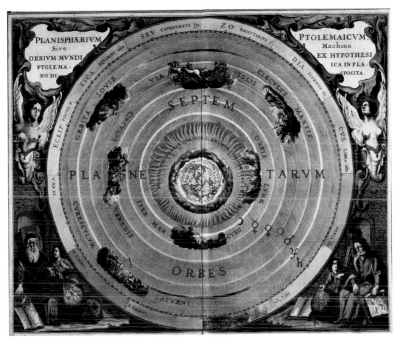

This engraving of the Ptolemaic solar system shows the model that was accepted as fact for more than a thousand years.

(*The Greatest*), created a picture of the solar system that was accepted as fact for more than one thousand years. In fact, Ptolemy's star chart of forty-eight constellations and the names he gave to many of those star groupings persist today.

It was not Ptolemy's star chart, however, that had the most impact on astronomy. His mathematical formulas were much more important in supporting the geocentric dogma of the church. Ptolemy supposedly proved the theory with pages of complex calculations that used geometry—a branch of mathematics that pertains to the measurements of points, lines, surfaces, circles, and angles. He also used a more advanced branch of mathematics, called trigonometry, which utilizes triangulation to calculate great distances. Using complex geometrical constructions, Ptolemy believed that he had explained the movement of celestial bodies.

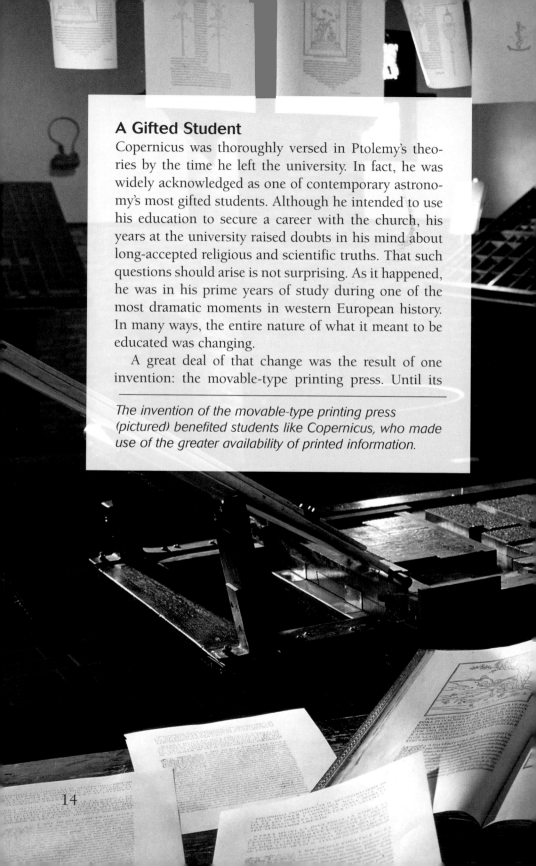

A Gifted Student

Copernicus was thoroughly versed in Ptolemy's theories by the time he left the university. In fact, he was widely acknowledged as one of contemporary astronomy's most gifted students. Although he intended to use his education to secure a career with the church, his years at the university raised doubts in his mind about long-accepted religious and scientific truths. That such questions should arise is not surprising. As it happened, he was in his prime years of study during one of the most dramatic moments in western European history. In many ways, the entire nature of what it meant to be educated was changing.

A great deal of that change was the result of one invention: the movable-type printing press. Until its

The invention of the movable-type printing press (pictured) benefited students like Copernicus, who made use of the greater availability of printed information.

invention in 1454, books that had been copied by hand were passed down from generation to generation. In fact, a good deal of a college student's education before the invention of the printing press consisted of copying ancient texts, usually in Latin, and learning by rote. With the printing press, however, books on a variety of topics could be quickly printed and widely distributed. As a result of this revolutionary invention, there were not only more books available to those who could read, there was more information to be read.

Much of the new information was collected at university libraries, including the one at Krakow. Because of this, Copernicus, who used a church-approved text that was hundreds of years old for his astronomy course, was also able to update what was known about the subject with new research and new resources. Unlike earlier students, he was also able to read contemporary criticisms of astrology as science, such as scholar Giovanni Pico della Mirandola's *Disputations Against Divinatory Astrology*, which, many years later, Copernicus noted having read in 1496. In *On the Revolution of the Celestial Orbs*, he also noted purchasing astronomy books published in 1490 and 1492 that offered current information on the topic.

Among the works Copernicus purchased was a guide to Ptolemy's *Almagest* written by German astronomer Georg von Peuerbach and his student Johann Müller, also called Regiomontanus. The guide was essentially a series of mathematical corrections to errors the two men had discovered in Ptolemy's work. This was Copernicus's first exposure to the work of scholars who did not blindly accept the prevailing beliefs of the time but instead sought to prove or disprove them in a scientific way.

A New View of the World

New scientific information about astronomy took on greater importance than ever during the years Copernicus attended college. In 1492, while Copernicus was in his second year of studies, Christopher Columbus sailed to North America, a continent that was previously unknown in Europe. His journey set off a flurry of voyages across open, uncharted ocean waters. A sudden need arose to plot ships' courses and determine locations beyond

As explorers voyaged farther from the known world, navigators, like the one depicted in this painting, used astronomical knowledge to chart ships' courses.

the sight of land. Knowledge of stars and planetary movement was necessary for this type of navigation.

In addition to the newfound significance of astronomy and geography, the nature of learning in general changed throughout universities—and society in general. Since the Middle Ages, the church had exercised complete control in public morals, education, literature, and the arts. Laws, books, artwork, and what was taught by educators all had to be approved by the church.

With the increased availability of books, however, teachers and students were no longer content to rely solely upon church-approved information. Instead, there was an increased demand for educational and creative freedoms. This period was the beginning of a century-long inquiry into ideas and flowering of culture that came to be known as the Renaissance.

During the Renaissance, people such as the humanist scholar Erasmus (pictured) demanded freedom from the intellectual restraints imposed by the church.

While the Renaissance was a time of great advances in science, literature, and the arts, it was also a period of great conflict between traditional Christians and humanists, who favored a more open society. Many humanists demanded freedom from the intellectual and moral restraints imposed by the church, and their work often highlighted what they interpreted as religious hypocrisy. Traditional Christians, on the other hand, considered humanists to be immoral people who had no place in civilized European society.

Copernicus, who, like many well-educated men of his time, was sympathetic to the humanist point of view, found himself caught between the two opposing groups. He saw no danger to the church from a discussion about religious traditions. For that reason, he felt he had an individual right to pursue knowledge wherever it led. On the other hand, he never doubted the faith in which he was raised, and he disagreed with those who considered the church a corrupt and hypocritical organization.

Copernicus chose to study at the University of Bologna because it had a respected reputation for astronomy. The tower of the university (pictured) served as an observatory.

Study in Italy

Still caught between the two opposing philosophies and uncertain about his future, Copernicus returned to Toruń in 1496 without a formal degree from Krakow. This, however, was not due to a lack of diligence. It was a common practice at the time for students to nearly finish their studies at one university, then complete the final requirements at another that had lower tuition. Following this custom, Copernicus withdrew from the University of Krakow with his uncle's approval and requested that he be allowed to complete his studies at the University of Bologna, in Italy.

At the time, Italy was not a unified nation; instead it was a loose assembly of city-states, including Bologna. Although Rome was the most famous city in Italy, it was the resident city of the pope and the center of the Church, while many other city-states were centers of humanist thought. Among the city-state most in favor of intellectual freedom and most opposed to the church was Bologna. One reason Copernicus hoped to continue his studies in Bologna was that it had a widely respected reputation for astronomy. Copernicus also wanted to expand his education to make himself more valuable for church service. For that reason, he also decided to pursue a degree in religious, or canon, law.

In the autumn of 1496, Copernicus entered the University of Bologna for three years of study. Because he had been considered an outstanding astronomy student at Krakow, he was able to procure room and board in the home of Domenico Maria de Novara, a mathematics and astrology professor. Among the tasks that de Novara performed at the university was the determination of which days religious holidays would fall upon. He also made predictions based upon his knowledge of astrology. His annual message provided the date on which Easter fell, as well as the dates of the phases of the moon, the dates of eclipses, and various auspicious or ominous dates in the coming year. He also made weather forecasts.

Despite de Novara's role as the university astrologer and weather forecaster, he did not blindly accept the teachings approved by the church. In private, he criticized the accuracy of Ptolemy's long-accepted "proof" of the geocentric theory. Although Copernicus was only in his early twenties and had not yet developed his own heliocentric theory, he could not help but be influenced in his thinking by de Novara, who was one of the most honored astronomers of his time. De Novara's doubts about Ptolemy's work—which had been generally accepted for centuries—made a profound impression on Copernicus. In the volume of *On the Revolution of the Celestial Orbs* that focuses on the Moon, Copernicus wrote that it was while he studied under de Novara that he developed his initial theory that the Moon was a satellite of Earth.

As influential as de Novara's thinking was on Copernicus, it was the older man's vast technical knowledge of astronomy that convinced Copernicus to become his protégé for three years. While Copernicus had already reached an advanced level of

Developed by the Greeks and Muslims, the astrolabe was the most important astronomical device of Copernicus's time.

mathematical knowledge, his comprehension of the specialized aspects of astronomy was still in the beginning stages. Under de Novara's tutelage, for example, Copernicus had to learn to master the basic tool of astronomical observation, the astrolabe.

The astrolabe was invented by the Greeks and more fully developed by Muslims during the Middle Ages. It made its first appearance in western Europe in the fourteenth century and immediately became the most important astronomical device. Most astrolabes consist of a balanced metal disk about six inches

In 1497, Copernicus became the canon at the Frombork cathedral (pictured). This position guaranteed him a lifetime income and time to pursue his astronomical research.

in diameter, which, when suspended by a ring, hangs perfectly vertical. One side of the disk is engraved with several circles divided into different categories, such as 360 degrees for a circle, 365.25 parts for the days of the year, and 12 divisions for the months of the year.

The other side of the plate is engraved with an outer circle of twenty-four divisions for the hours of the day. Another circle, used as a calendar, is inscribed with the signs of the zodiac and shows the Sun's position for every day of the year. Openings cut into this circle form a map of the night sky and divide it into individual constellations. Several "tongues" or "flames" cut into the disk point to important stars. By adjusting either side of the disk, it is possible for an astronomer to determine the time of day or night or the time of the year, and also predict the arrangement of planets and stars on a specific date. As a navigation tool, the astrolabe can be used to determine latitude and the direction of the North Star.

Using the astrolabe, de Novara showed Copernicus how the star Aldebaran would disappear behind a shadow cast by the moon on March 8, 1497. The eclipse occurred as predicted, and Copernicus later recalled the event as a defining moment in his decision to pursue astronomy regardless of any other career demands.

In the same way that his introduction to the work of Peuerbach had introduced him to rigorous mathematical review of accepted facts, Copernicus's study under a scholar like de Novara strengthened his belief that long-accepted theories should be treated skeptically until proven. As the fifteenth century drew to a close, his doubts about the geocentric theory emerged for the first time.

A Position in the Church

While he flourished as an astronomer under de Novara, Copernicus was also diligent in the study of subjects that would further his career in the church. His hard work was rewarded in 1497, when Copernicus received word that he had been appointed to serve in Frombork, Poland, as canon, or administrator, of the Ermeland diocese. A diocese is a regional area governed by a bishop of the church, in this case, Copernicus's uncle. Thanks to the efforts of his uncle, he was now essentially guaranteed an income and a residence for life. By this time, the twenty-six-year-old Copernicus had decided that he would devote his life to learning, and the position of canon at the Frombork cathedral allowed him sufficient time to pursue his astronomical research.

Although canons were prohibited from marriage and lived on church property, they were not priests. Instead, they were administrative employees of the church who also assisted in religious services and sang in choirs. Because the church was also a governing institution, men trained in the administration of civil, religious, and criminal law were needed in every diocese. Canons carried out these services, and they also wrote contracts, oversaw church property, and performed other clerical tasks. In some cases, canons received medical training and provided health care to the priests in the diocese.

Study of Medicine

Copernicus did not assume his position of canon immediately after he received the appointment. In fact, aware that he would have to settle down when he returned to Poland, Copernicus was in no rush to leave Italy. In 1500, he traveled to Rome for the jubilee, a celebration of the church that was held every twenty-five years. Although he intended to stay for only a brief time, his reputation as a rising young scholar preceded him, and, with his uncle's permission, he remained in Rome for a year and taught mathematics and astronomy. While he was there, he predicted and observed an eclipse of the moon. He also became increasingly fascinated by what he observed in the sky with his naked eye and spent his free time sketching the positions of the constellations and planets.

Copernicus could not, however, avoid his canonical responsibilities forever. In the spring of 1501, he returned to Frombork to be officially installed as a canon for the Ermeland diocese. Despite his official title, he had not completed work on his canon law degree. Once again, Copernicus wished to further his education. He appealed to his uncle, who was now elderly, and asked to be allowed to return to Italy to complete the degree. Copernicus also requested permission to begin degree work in

This engraving depicts Copernicus as he observes a lunar eclipse. In 1500, while in Rome, Copernicus predicted and observed such an eclipse.

the study of medicine. Copernicus's uncle, who hoped to have his nephew as his personal physician, granted him leave in 1501. In a letter to Copernicus's supervisors, Waczenrode wrote that he granted permission to his nephew not out of favoritism, but "principally because Nicolaus promised to study medicine, and as a helpful physician would some day advise . . . the members of the [diocese]."[3]

Once again, Copernicus went to Italy. To complete his studies, he went to the university in the city-state of Padua. Copernicus chose Padua over Bologna for two reasons. The university in Padua was famous for its medical school, and while he was there, Copernicus would be able to pursue further study in

The oldest medical manuscript in existence is at the University of Padua, where Copernicus studied medicine in 1501.

astronomy. At the time, the astrological component of astronomy was considered to be a key element in medicine, since a good deal of medical diagnosis and treatment was based on astrological information.

Medical treatment, for example, often depended upon whether it was a favorable day to perform a procedure. If not, treatment would be postponed until the signs were more positive. In addition, each sign of the zodiac was believed to rule a different part of the human body. For example, Sagittarius controlled the thighs, and Pisces, the feet. Medical texts in Copernicus's time contained a diagram of a man to show which parts of the body were controlled by corresponding signs of the zodiac.

The connection between the zodiac and the moon determined whether the practice of bleeding—draining blood from the part of the body that was affected —would be beneficial. Exactly when a patient would benefit most from bleeding was dictated by the phase and the position of the

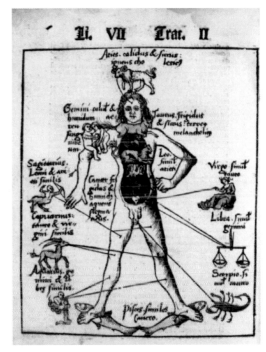

When Copernicus studied medicine, each sign of the zodiac was believed to rule a different part of the human body.

moon. For example, if the moon was in the sign of the zodiac that ruled a particular part of the body, bloodletting from that area was to be avoided, because the attraction of the moon was believed to cause excessive bleeding. Medical texts also showed when the phases of the moon changed.

Return to Poland

While he studied medicine, Copernicus took additional courses in law. By the spring of 1503, he had completed enough coursework to receive a doctorate in canon law. He remained in Padua to continue his study of medicine, but he left before he received his medical degree. Instead of taking up his position at Frombork, he was granted leave from his official law duties to serve as his uncle's private physician.

For the next decade, Copernicus lived with his uncle, the bishop of Ermeland, in his residence at Healdsburg Castle, a few miles from Frombork. In addition to caring for him and other church officials, Copernicus also performed free medical services for the poor in the surrounding region. His duties, however, extended beyond health care. He essentially became his uncle's private secretary and personal astrologer as well.

While his role as an astrologer afforded him time to observe the skies and note the position of celestial bodies, his life of service left him little time to pursue the painstaking mathematical component of astronomy. What little free time he had was spent in less demanding scholarly pursuits. For example, he translated a book of letters and essays by the Greek philosopher Theophylactus into Latin. The book was published in 1509.

After the translation was published, Copernicus remained in service to his uncle until 1512, when Waczenrode died. Copernicus returned to Frombork, where he resumed his duties as canon for the diocese. Freed of his medical responsibilities, he now had a considerable amount of time to devote to astronomy. Copernicus moved into rooms in one of the towers in the town's fortifications, where he set up an observatory.

The Power of the Church

Although his career allowed him to continue his observations, Copernicus's decision to serve the church came at a time when Christianity was entering a period of great unrest. For centuries, the church had been the most powerful political, military, and religious force in Europe. The pope had been considered to be infallible—incapable of making an error in any of the church's actions or decisions—from the earliest days of the church.

Few nations existed in the Middle Ages or Renaissance that could stand up to the power of the church. Its unrivaled authority, however, caused a great deal of resentment among the people of certain regions, and that same authority led to abuses of power by some church leaders who used their position for personal benefit.

Among the most egregious abuses of power by the church were those that occurred in Germany and Poland during the

After he returned to Frombork in 1512, Copernicus set up this observatory in a tower of one of the town's fortifications.

1400s. Trial and execution for religious reasons was not uncommon. During this period, for example, thousands of people were put to death for witchcraft. It was thought that witches could not only change shape and fly but were also involved in a plot to overthrow the church. The church reaped great riches from these

During the Spanish Inquisition, depicted in this painting, church leaders severely punished those who refused to convert to Christianity.

trials because the pope decreed that the property of anyone who was convicted of witchcraft belonged to the church.

Witch hunts of different sorts took place throughout Europe as the fifteenth century came to an end. In Spain, the Inquisition was conducted by church leaders who sought to convert all non-believers to Christianity. Those who did not submit to conversion were burned at the stake. The church acquired great wealth in Spain. In fact, one of the richest church leaders was Cardinal Rodrigo Borgia of Valencia, who in 1492 became the man who is widely considered to be the most corrupt pope ever to lead the church.

Known as Pope Alexander VI, Borgia manipulated his election to the papacy through bribery of the church leaders, called cardinals, who voted for him. Once elected, he sold leadership positions, such as cardinalships and bishoprics, for huge sums of money. Alexander VI's ten years in power were spent in pursuit of his family's enrichment. In 1502, he died after being poisoned by a disgruntled follower.

Pope Alexander VI, considered the most corrupt pope ever to lead the church, enjoyed ten years in power before his murder in 1502.

During Alexander VI's papacy, Copernicus attended several universities in Italy that openly questioned the pope's rule and the behavior of other officials at the highest levels of the church. The doubts that many people expressed about the infallibility of the pope paralleled Copernicus's doubts about the church-

Copernicus's job as canon allowed him time to observe and record the movements of the stars and planets.

approved geocentric theory. His doubts had begun as vague uncertainty ten years before and grown stronger under de Novara. By the early 1500s, he was torn between his unquestioning devotion to the church—and his uncle—and his keen scientific intellect that accepted nothing on faith alone. Nevertheless, he returned to Poland, the scene of numerous witchcraft trials, to work as a canon. He did so fully aware that anyone who broke with church teachings or law risked torture and death.

First Works in Astronomy

Although Copernicus was involved with the church, he had little to do with the political or religious workings of it. Initially, his low-level clerical job perfectly suited him, because he had enough spare time to observe and record the movement of stars and planets from his observatory. In 1514, he handwrote and distributed—to a few close friends—a book that has come to be known as the *Little Commentary*. Although the work contained no mathematical calculations, it was the first known appearance in writing of Copernicus's heliocentric theory.

The *Little Commentary* is a valuable document because it contains what are known as the seven axioms. These statements form the basis of all of Copernicus's astronomical research. His conclusions, he explained, would be based on these statements, which he intended to prove:

There is no one center of the universe.

Earth is not the center of the universe.

The center of the planetary system is the sun.

The distance from Earth to the sun is miniscule compared with the distance to the stars.

The daily rotation of the stars is actually caused by Earth's rotation.

The annual movement of the sun across the sky is caused by Earth revolving around the sun.

With the Sun at the center of the solar system, planets farther from the Sun move more slowly in their orbits than do planets that are closer, and so appear to pass the slower-moving planets in retrograde motion.

Although the first six axioms had been discussed in one form or another among some astronomers, nobody before Copernicus had correctly explained the retrograde motion of the outer planets. Retrograde motion is the phenomenon that causes a planet to appear to move backward instead of traveling in its normal path. Occasionally, a planet will appear to undergo retrograde motion for a brief period of one or two days.

For more than a thousand years, astronomers had accepted Ptolemy's explanation for the phenomenon of retrograde motion. In his geocentric system, retrograde motion occurs when a planet, while it orbits Earth, also revolves in a smaller circle called an epicycle, much like the moon revolves around Earth. At certain points in the epicycle, according to Ptolemy, planets move from east to west, even as the center of the epicycle continues its west-to-east orbit.

Copernicus rejected Ptolemy's epicycle model in the Little Commentaries. Copernicus's explanation for retrograde motion conforms to a widely accepted principle of physics. For example, when the faster-moving Earth passes the slower-moving Mars, Mars appears to move backward.

Copernicus based his explanation of retrograde motion primarily on his observations and calculations of the movements of Mars. Like most astronomers of his time, Copernicus observed the sky by creating imaginary dividing lines that separated the area overhead into segments. The imaginary line directly overhead that divided the sky into halves, for example, was called the celestial equator. By separating the sky into segments, an astronomer could track, record, and measure any change in location made by a celestial body over a period of time.

The main instrument Copernicus used to keep precise track of the motion of the celestial bodies was the armillary sphere, which, next to the astrolabe, was the most common astronomical tool of the time. Copernicus did all of his calculations at a desk with an armillary sphere at his side. The tool resembles a hollow globe that sits in a cuplike holder. It is a model of the celestial sphere based on the viewpoint of the observer. The sphere is formed by rings, called armillae, which represent the circular paths of celestial bodies that move across the sky during the course of a year in relation to the observer, to the horizon, and to the celestial equator. Each armilla is measured in scales on the rings that indicate a body's movement over the course of a year.

Although Copernicus's conclusion about retrograde motion was drawn from observations of just one planet, it was a simple explanation of what was essentially an optical illusion—albeit one that had confused astronomers for centuries—and could be used to explain all retrograde motion. For those who believed in the heliocentric theory, Copernicus's explanation of retrograde motion served as irrefutable evidence in favor of it.

Few who accepted his theory, however, could wholeheartedly advocate it without conclusive mathematical proof. Copernicus understood that reluctance. While the *Little Commentary* showed evidence of an enormous amount of time and thought, he knew that the book was only a first step in proving his theory. In the introduction to the book, he wrote, "Here, for the sake of brevity, I have thought it desirable to omit the mathematical demonstrations intended for my larger work."[4]

After his seven axioms received general approval among the small group he trusted, Copernicus proceeded with his painstak-

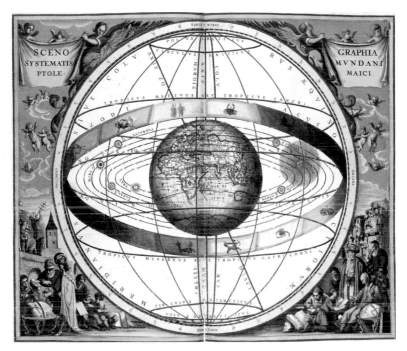

In his Little Commentary, *Copernicus rejected Ptolemy's epicycle model of retrograde motion (pictured).*

ing observations, which he recorded and measured constantly with his astrolabe and armillary sphere. From 1514 on, the meticulous observations and calculations he made were used to prove his axioms in his masterwork *On the Revolution of the Celestial Orbs*.

As Copernicus was completing work on the *Little Commentaries*, the pope requested that he join other reputable astronomers in Rome to improve and recalculate the church calendar, which had been in use since the days of the Roman Empire more than one thousand years before.

After the time Copernicus spent in Rome as a teacher, his reputation as an astronomer was highly respected by church leaders in Rome. The esteem in which he was held, however, was based mainly on his reputation as an astrologer.

The invitation came about because early Christian calendars had been based on the Hebrew lunar calendar, which had a cycle

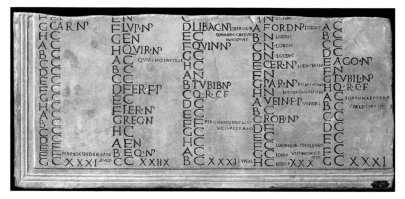

Copernicus refused the pope's request that he improve and recalculate the thousand-year-old Roman calendar (pictured).

of twenty-eight days. Over time, it had become increasingly difficult to accurately set the days on which holidays and other religious observances would fall because years were measured by the progression of the sun across the sky. As the years passed, a lunar year of 336 days and a solar year of 365 days yielded different dates for holiday. Because the date of the main Christian holiday of Easter depended on the date of the Hebrew festival of Passover, it had become increasingly confusing to establish on which date Easter fell.

The confusion over Easter was not the only concern of the church. The astrological facet of the calendar had become undependable as well. Church leaders had begun to doubt the reliability of forecasts for favorable days for medical procedures, as well as for agricultural activities such as plowing, sowing, and harvesting.

Many astronomers, who were by and large astrologers, were honored by the pope's request and went to Rome to adjust the calendar. Copernicus, however, refused to be involved. In a letter to the pope, he said he had no desire to engage in discussions on the calendar because the movement of heavenly bodies was still not truly understood by science.

Copernicus's research into planetary and solar motion consisted mainly of his observations of Mars and the Sun. His calculations suggested that the Sun's daily path across the sky had moved by more thirty degrees since the time of Ptolemy. This indicated to him that even the measurement of the solar, or sidereal year, was far from accurate.

Although he was not disciplined by the curch for his refusal, Copernicus took a risk by voicing his doubts about church-approved theory. For a man who depended on the church for his livelihood to question the accuracy of the centuries-old geocentric theory was extremely bold. In his daily life, Copernicus may have been a quiet church canon, but as he devoted more and more time to astronomy, he became increasingly firm in his personal beliefs about the structure of the universe.

Luther's Historic Challenge

Personal beliefs, whether in matters of science or faith, played a large role in events that changed Europe in the 1500s. While Copernicus was one of the few astronomers to question accepted church ideology regarding celestial motion, he was not the only person who questioned the authority of the church. In 1517, while Copernicus was temporarily serving as a canon in Olsztyn, a fortress near Frombork, a German monk who was slightly younger than he challenged the church in a way that had a much more immediate and divisive impact. The monk's name was Martin Luther, and his challenge created a dramatic division among the followers of the church.

Luther's challenge came about after a long period in which many Christians began to raise questions about the power of the pope and church leaders. Although Luther had been a monk since the early 1500s, he questioned some of the practices of the church. A devoutly religious man, Luther had come to believe that the pope and other high church leaders were more interested in power and wealth than in matters of religious faith. In particular, Luther felt that the popes had been overly involved in Italian political matters. Corruption during the reign of Pope Alexander VI had also raised doubts about the infallibility of the pope.

In the second decade of the sixteenth century, the church began to sell indulgences, which was a method of raising money from faithful Christians to pay for, among other things, paintings, sculpture, and cathedrals in Rome. Indulgences were purchased

Martin Luther challenged the integrity of church leadership. His followers became known as Protestants while those loyal to the pope were known as Catholics.

by Christians to free themselves from the obligation of following church law. For example, a person who wanted to eat meat on Friday instead of fish, which church law required, could buy an indulgence from a church official and be forgiven of the sin.

By 1517, church leaders had declared that it was possible to buy indulgences for more serious sins, such as those listed in the Ten Commandments. Indulgences could be bought, Christians were told, that would assure entry into heaven after death, no matter what sins the person had committed during his or her lifetime. This led to the practice of selling indulgences to people to secure a place in heaven for family members who had already died. Although most of the money raised through the sale of indulgences paid for artwork and church buildings in Italy, some was used to pay the salaries of church administrators, and some was kept by corrupt churchmen.

In late 1517, Luther publicly questioned the integrity of the leadership of the church. On November 1, he wrote a long list of criticisms about the practice of selling indulgences and nailed it to the door of the church in Wittenberg, Germany. Luther objected to indulgences on the grounds that only God could forgive a Christian's sins. By doing so, Luther implicitly rejected the divine authority and the infallibility of the pope. Luther also wrote that a religious person could reach heaven through a direct relationship with God and that no church authority was needed to do so. He also questioned the church's concepts of confession and

Money raised from the selling of indulgences paid for church buildings and artwork.

prayer to saints. Luther's break with the church had a revolutionary impact upon Christians almost immediately.

Within a short time, Germany, Poland, and much of the rest of Europe was enveloped in the turmoil resulting from Luther's actions at Wittenberg. Luther found great support among Germans who agreed that the indulgences had corrupted the church and who preferred a direct relationship with God rather than through the pope and other church leaders.

Eventually, Luther's followers left the church and became known as Protestants; those who were loyal to the pope became known as Catholics. The rise of Protestantism created a divide in Christianity that has lasted for hundreds of years. The division led to a long period of wars between Protestants and Catholics. Violence spread across Europe until it eventually reached Frombork, where Copernicus was occupied with his astronomical research.

A Decade of Research

By the early 1520s, Copernicus hoped for nothing more than peace and quiet to make observations and to work out his heliocentric theory. Unfortunately for him, the conflict between Protestants and Catholics resulted in a series of attacks on Catholic fortresses in Poland by a group of mercenary German soldiers known as the Teutonic Knights. German attackers placed Olsztyn, a town near Frombork, under siege, and Copernicus took command of the defense of Olsztyn at the request of the townspeople. For a period of three years in the early 1520s, until the attackers withdrew, Copernicus supervised the siege defenses around Olsztyn.

Despite his military responsibilities, Copernicus managed to continue his observatory work during the winter months when, as was the practice, military activity ceased. By this time, his research had proved that the sun's arc across the sky changed from year to year, as did the point at which it was the greatest distance from Earth. Rather than blindly follow the mathematical path that Ptolemy had taken, Copernicus applied trigonometry to calculate the distances he measured. His results flew in the face of the predictable consistency suggested by Ptolemy's work.

Copernicus observed and measured Venus, Mars, and Jupiter (upper right), as well as Saturn, for four years.

When Copernicus compared his measurements of the annual movement made by the Sun with his previous records and with the records of earlier astronomers, he discovered that the distances changed from year to year. Copernicus's observations of the relative distances between Earth and the sun led him to another of his revolutionary breakthroughs: Earth wobbles like a top on its axis as it orbits the Sun.

By 1523, Copernicus had completed much of the work necessary to substantiate his theory of Earth's movement. He spent the next year observing the Moon, tracking its cycles as it moved through segments of the sky and recording its movement on the armillary sphere. In the end, he reached another revolutionary conclusion: the Moon orbited Earth rather than the Sun.

Copernicus realized he would have to apply the same methods of observation to the other celestial bodies.

Copernicus devoted four years to the observation and measurement of Saturn, Jupiter, Venus, and Mercury—the planets that, in addition to Mars, are visible to the naked eye. By 1530,

During the 1520s and 1530s, Copernicus lived in the monastery and administered the property owned by the diocese in and around Frombork.

he had almost completed the first draft of all six volumes of *On the Revolution of the Celestial Orbs*. As a scientist, however, Copernicus felt strongly that all of his work had to be repeated and checked before it would be ready to publish. In addition, he understood how revolutionary his astronomical theories were and was reluctant to challenge the accepted wisdom of the Catholic Church.

Canonical Responsibilities

As important as his theories were to him, Copernicus's main responsibility was to the Catholic Church. Without his salary and the living quarters at Frombork provided by the church, he would have had to seek employment at a university. Although he had taught intermittently over the years, he felt a loyalty to the diocese.

Throughout the 1520s and early 1530s, Copernicus administered much of the property owned by the diocese in and around Frombork. Some of the land had been confiscated during the witchcraft trials and was leased to tenant farmers. Copernicus collected rent in his role of administrator, managed military preparedness, controlled the diocese's finances, and oversaw the church's bakery, brewery, and mills. He also cared for the medical needs of the other canons and local residents.

Because of his versatility and stamina, Copernicus was highly regarded for his ability to fulfill his canonical duties. In fact, his reputation as a financial manager was such that he served as an economic adviser to Duke Albert, who was the ruler of Prussia. Copernicus instituted monetary policies that prevented prices from becoming inflated, and published several economic texts. During the 1520s, he also represented the duke in meetings with the leaders of other provinces.

As a canon, Copernicus had never been required to take the religious vows required of priests. In early 1531, however, the bishop of Frombork insisted that Copernicus take the vows. In the aftermath of the split in the church, Catholic leaders in Rome wanted canons to take the priestly vows as a demonstration of their loyalty to the faith. If Copernicus refused to do so, the bishop threatened, Copernicus would lose his salary and be forced to find his own living quarters.

Instead of publishing it, Copernicus (center) decided to orally present his heliocentric theory to some of his closest colleagues.

By this time, Copernicus had served the diocese for almost twenty years and had no interest in pursuing a religious position, so he refused the order. He was held in such high regard, however, that the bishop was afraid to lose his economic expertise. The demand was overlooked, and Copernicus, nearly sixty years old, resumed his dual career as canon and astronomer.

Sharing the Theory

By late 1531, Copernicus had completed work on his version of the heliocentric theory, but he was far from certain that he wanted to publish it. Instead, he considered an alternative: an oral presentation of his theory to his closest colleagues. To assist these chosen few, he contemplated the addition of new information to the material he had published in the *Little Commentaries*.

By the early 1530s, Copernicus's theory of the heliocentric system had spread across Europe by word of mouth. Some of the more liberal officials of the Catholic Church expressed interest in his ideas. In 1533, a German astronomer, Albert Widmanstadt, presented the theory to Pope Clement VII. The pope dismissed the theory but did not condemn those who believed it. In 1536, a group of cardinals in Rome actually urged Copernicus to publish his work.

Copernicus, however, was still not prepared to release his life's work to the world. He understood that his view of the universe would upset many people. Luther, for example, was one of many who refused to accept Copernicus's theory because it contradicted the Bible. In 1539, he called Copernicus "a fool who wants to turn the entire science of astronomy upside down! But, as the Bible tells us, Joshua told the sun, not the Earth, to stop in its path!"[5]

Pope Clement VII, one of the more liberal officials of the Catholic Church, did not condemn those who believed Copernicus's theory.

Rhäticus Arrives

Not all Germans—or all Protestants—were as dismissive of Copernicus as Luther. In the 1530s, a young German mathematics professor heard of Copernicus's theories and decided he had to go to Frombork. His name was Georg Rhäticus.

As a Protestant, Rhäticus knew he would risk his life if he went to Frombork, a Catholic stronghold. Tensions from Luther's break with the church and the corresponding split in Christianity remained high even after twenty years. In addition, Rhäticus's father, a doctor and an astrologer, had been tried by the church for witchcraft and beheaded when Georg was fourteen. Rhäticus had grown up in great fear of the church but went to Frombork in 1539 anyway.

Rhäticus was twenty-five when he first met Copernicus, who was then sixty-six. The younger man, who held a secure position at the University of Wittenberg, had taken a leave of absence from the university to study under Copernicus, whom he had never met. Nevertheless, he wrote in a letter, he made the decision easily: "I heard of . . . Copernicus . . . and although the University of Wittenberg had made me a public professor . . . I did not think that I should be content until I had learned something more through the instruction of that man. And I also say that I regret neither the financial expenses nor the long journey nor the remaining hardships."[6]

By the time Rhäticus arrived, *On the Revolution of the Celestial Orbs* had been completed for almost ten years. At the same time that some European astronomers debated the theory, Copernicus continued to recheck his calculations and observations. Rhäticus noted that Copernicus was extremely meticulous in his scientific methods. He described Copernicus at work:

> My teacher always had before his eyes the observations of all ages together with his own, assembled in order. . . . [When] some conclusion must be drawn . . . he proceeds from the earliest observations to his own . . . and having made a most careful . . . rejection . . .he assumes new hypotheses . . . by applying mathematics, [and] geometrically establishes the conclusions which can be drawn . . . and after performing all these operations he finally writes down the laws of astronomy.[7]

Rhäticus Examines the Work

For his part, Copernicus was pleased to have someone to review his work closely. He turned over to Rhäticus his life's astronomical research, which he had compiled into six volumes written in Latin and called *De Revolutionibus Orbium Coelestium*, or *On the Revolution of the Celestial Orbs*. The volumes were structured much like Ptolemy's *Almagest*. In *On the Revolution of the Celestial*

Georg Rhäticus was eager to review On the Revolution of the Celestial Orbs, *Copernicus's six-volume compilation of his astronomical research.*

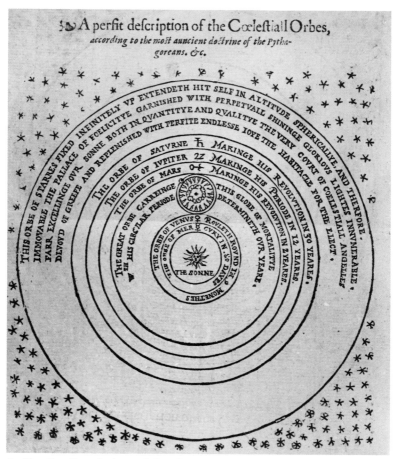

In On the Revolution of the Celestial Orbs, *Copernicus presented his heliocentric theory of the solar system.*

Orbs's first volume, Copernicus stated his hypotheses and added, "I shall treat many topics differently from my predecessors, and yet I shall do so [with] thanks to them, for it was they who first opened the road to the investigation of these very questions."[8] Copernicus then went on to briefly discuss the ideas that he had stated in his previous book, *Little Commentaries*, in 1514.

After a short essay on each of the seven earlier axioms from the work, he concluded that "all these facts are disclosed . . . by the principle . . . in which the planets follow one another, and by the harmony of the entire universe, if only we look at the matter, as the saying goes, with both eyes."[9] He then suggested the following arrangement of celestial bodies:

> The first and the highest of all is the sphere of the fixed stars, which contains itself and everything, and is therefore immovable. It is unquestionably the place of the universe, to which the motion and position of all the other heavenly bodies are compared. . . . The sphere of the fixed stars is followed by the first of the planets, Saturn, which completes its circuit in thirty years. After Saturn, Jupiter accomplishes its revolution in twelve years. Then Mars revolves in two years. The annual revolution takes the series' fourth place, which contains the earth . . . together with the lunar sphere as an epicycle. In the fifth place Venus returns in nine months. Lastly, the sixth place is held by Mercury, which revolves in a period of 80 days.[10]

At the end of the first volume, Copernicus presents the most revolutionary component of his theory: "At rest, however, in the middle of everything is the sun, for in this most beautiful temple, who would place this lamp in another or better position than that from which it can light up the whole at the same time. For the sun is called by some people the lantern of the universe, its mind by others end its ruler by still others."[11]

Copernicus concluded the first book of *On the Revolution of the Celestial Orbs* by admitting that his theory would be difficult for many people to accept. He wrote that his statements "are difficult and almost inconceivable, being of course opposed to the beliefs of many people . . . [but] as we proceed, with God's help I shall make them clearer than sunlight, at any rate to those who are not unacquainted with the science of astronomy."[12]

Narratio Prima
By late 1539, Rhäticus had carefully reviewed Copernicus's first volume and was eager to see it published. Copernicus was ready to present to the world his view of the order of the planets and

how to calculate the distances of the planets from the sun. With Copernicus's permission, Rhäticus added a preface to the work that supported Copernicus's methods and conclusion.

In the preface, Rhäticus compares Copernicus's theory of the universe to the complex mechanisms of a clock. For his part, Copernicus compares his predecesors' theories to a drawing of a human figure in which the arms, legs, and head were put together so haphazardly that the result was a monster. His theory of the universe, he says, is one in which a change in the position of any part of its makeup would disrupt the perfection of the whole.

The first volume of *On the Revolution of the Celestial Orbs* was complete enough in its description of Copernicus's heliocentric theory that it could alone stand as a publication. Because he believed so strongly in Copernicus and wanted to get the theory printed and distributed as quickly as possible, Rhäticus undertook the responsibility of finding someone to pay for the cost of publishing the first volume. Rhäticus returned to Germany and approached the mayor of Gdańsk a large port city that was a Protestant stronghold. The mayor read the book and agreed to pay for its publication. In early 1540, volume one was published as *Narratio Prima*. The favorable response to the book pleased Copernicus immensely. When Rhäticus returned to Frombork, Copernicus asked him to review all of the remaining volumes as well.

The Enthusiastic Student

Rhäticus eagerly took to the task of reviewing the other five volumes and began to closely inspect the twenty-five years of calculations that Copernicus had done. Many of the complex equations that establish Copernicus's proof of the heliocentric theory are contained in the second volume. In the third volume, Copernicus focuses on the movements of the Sun. It is here that he discusses the passage of the Sun across the sky that causes it to appear to move closer or farther away from Earth during the course of the year. In fact, as Copernicus explains, the opposite is true—it is Earth that changes position, not the Sun. This statement sets the stage for the remaining volumes of *On the Revolution of the Celestial Orbs*.

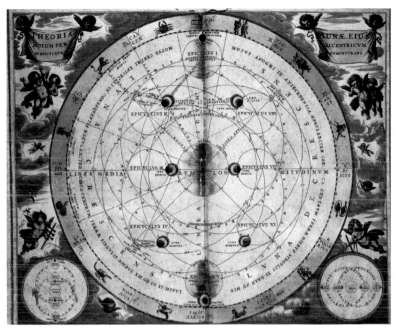

In the fourth volume of On the Revolution of the Celestial Orbs, *Copernicus proved that the Moon orbits Earth, and Earth orbits the Sun.*

The fourth volume of *On the Revolution of the Celestial Orbs* applies the conclusions made in the first three books to the movements made by the Moon. Copernicus proves that the Moon orbits Earth and that Earth orbits the Sun. As part of his explanation, he cites the lunar eclipse he had observed in 1497 in Bologna with de Novara. With each volume, Copernicus continues to compile evidence of celestial movement that supports his heliocentric theory.

The final two volumes follow the format of the first four. Volume five offers proof of the heliocentric theory that is based on the movements made by Mars, Saturn, and Jupiter, the planets farther from the Sun than Earth is. It is in this volume that Copernicus presents the detailed version of his theory pertaining to retrograde motion. His final volume, focuses on his observations of Mercury and Venus, the planets closer to the Sun than Earth is. The cumulative weight of this evidence and of the more

Copernicus spent thirty years methodically observing and recording data, as shown in this page from one of his manuscripts, to prove that Earth is not the center of the universe.

than thirty years of methodical observations, recording of data, and calculation establishes that Earth is not the center of the universe but merely one of the planets orbiting the Sun. After Rhäticus completed his review of volume six, only the lack of financing stood in the way of publishing the rest of *On the Revolution of the Celestial Orbs*.

Final Publication

By mid-1541, Copernicus and Rhäticus had worked together for more than two and a half years on the last five volumes. Copernicus was finally ready to turn over the rest of his writing for publication. Again, Rhäticus assumed responsibility for securing funds for publication. Because there was so much more to publish, however, the costs would be much higher.

Rhäticus decided to approach a person of wealth who was familiar with Copernicus and his abilities: Duke Albert, the ruler of Royal Prussia for whom Copernicus had worked as an economic adviser. In August 1541, Rhäticus presented Albert with an astrolabe that he had made. He assured the ruler that the device was as accurate as any instrument he had ever used in the determination of the exact hour of sunrise, a reading that had long interested the duke. Next, Rhäticus asked the ruler to pro vide funds to publish Copernicus's remaining volumes. Albert, long an admirer of Copernicus, quickly agreed. Afterward, Rhäticus traveled to Nuremberg, Germany, and took the manuscript to Johann Petreius, one of the most well-known printers of the day.

As it happened, however, Rhäticus was unable to stay to oversee Petreius's work. He learned he had lost his teaching position at the University of Wittenberg because of his public declarations of support for Copernicus's work. Without a job or an income, he was forced to travel to the distant city of Leipzig, Germany, to take a teaching position. He left the supervision of the printing to a Lutheran clergyman named Andreas Osiander. Although he was a church official, Osiander had considerable experience in the process of printing, especially with mathematical texts.

Like the majority of Protestant and Catholic clergy, Osiander was a firm believer in the geocentric theory. After he read through Copernicus's work, he felt he had to insert a comment about its conclusions. Osiander wrote an anonymous note to replace Copernicus's original introduction. The only part of Copernicus's preface that Osiander left untouched was the dedication of the book to the current pope, Paul III, a man known for his strong belief in astrology.

In his note, Osiander warns readers that astronomy is an inexact science and that the conclusions presented in the book are not actually proven. Instead, he wrote, the information Copernicus presented in the volumes offers a simpler way to calculate the positions of the heavenly bodies in the geocentric universe. Osiander wrote this preface without consulting either Copernicus or Rhäticus.

Rhäticus was astonished when he received his copy of the first printing. He became so angry that he crossed out the preface with a large red X, and immediately went to Nuremberg to confront Osiander. It was precisely because the work was so exact that the work was valuable, Rhäticus told Osiander. The new preface diminished its importance, said Rhäticus.

Osiander, who had been a Catholic priest before becoming a Protestant cleric, told the much younger Rhäticus that the conclusions presented in Copernicus's work were too revolutionary. To publish it without his note, Osiander said, would be too dangerous for all involved. With the note, he told Rhäticus, people would be able to read it without fear of being accused of violating religious principles.

Final Days

Rhäticus was unconvinced by Osiander's argument, but because of his new academic responsibilities in Leipzig, he was unable to return to Frombork until May 1543. By that time, Copernicus, now seventy, had suffered a series of strokes that paralyzed his right side and left him mute and bedridden. Rhäticus presented Copernicus with the first copy of *On the Revolution of the Celestial Orbs* on the day he died. Copernicus suffered a cerebral hemorrhage on May 24, 1543. He died in the observatory in Frombork, where he had spent so many hours observing the sky.

Whether the dying Copernicus understood what Osiander did is unknown. In fact, Osiander's insertion remained a closely guarded secret for more than sixty years. It was not until 1609 that the famous astronomer Johannes Kepler revealed publicly what Osiander had done and the original preface was recovered from Copernicus's papers and placed in new printings of *On the Revolution of the Celestial Orbs*.

The preface written by Copernicus was far different from the one that had been inserted by the Lutheran clergyman. In his preface, Copernicus addressed those would who criticize his conclusion: "Perhaps there will be babblers who, although

---

On his deathbed in 1543, Copernicus received the first printed copy of On the Revolution of the Celestial Orbs.

completely ignorant of mathematics, nevertheless take it upon themselves to pass judgment . . . and, badly distorting some passages of Scripture to their purpose, will dare find fault with my undertaking. . . . I disregard them. . . . Their criticism [is] unfounded,"[13] he wrote.

Immediate Aftermath

Osiander may have been correct in his assumption that his preface would help *On the Revolution of the Celestial Orb* to gain wider acceptance. Approximately one thousand copies of Copernicus's work were published in two printings in 1543 and 1566. Few of those who consulted the book considered themselves to be what became known as Copernicans. Most sixteenth-century astronomers consulted Copernicus's work because its calculations offered more accurate formulas for predicting the positions of planets, which in turn meant more precise astrological forecasts.

As useful as Copernicus's formulas were, his theories drew little outright support from scholars. As was the case with Rhäticus, most men affiliated with universities who spoke in favor of Copernicus lost their teaching positions. Organized religion, too, refused to change its dogma to accept the heliocentric theory. Protestants were the first to object to the Copernican theory, citing, as Luther did, the Bible. Protestant officials printed many pamphlets during the 1500s that condemned Copernicus not only as a fraud but also as a Catholic. The Catholic Church also moved against Copernicus's work. In the early 1600s, *On the Revolution of the Celestial Orbs* was banned, which means that Catholics were forbidden to read it. The prohibition lasted until 1758.

Under such antiheliocentric pressure, few scientists were willing to proclaim their belief in Copernicus's work. Between 1543 and 1625, fewer than ten astronomers publicly claimed to support the Copernican theory. The most famous of these Copernicans were Johannes Kepler and Galileo Galilei. These men, also

Galileo was sentenced to life in prison for being one of the few scientists to support Copernicus's heliocentric theory.

Copernicus showed that scientists were not fortune-tellers, helped separate astronomy from astrology, and blazed a trail for future scientific exploration.

considered giants of astronomy, suffered for their beliefs. Kepler was excommunicated by the Lutheran Church, and Galileo was sentenced to life in prison by the Catholic Church, although he was allowed to serve the sentence at his home.

The Reputation of Copernicus

Despite his meticulous work and the support of such important figures as Kepler and Galileo, Copernicus's theory actually contains numerous errors. The universe is not a sphere, for example, and the orbits of planets are not the perfect circles that Copernicus attempted to prove they were.

Nevertheless, Copernicus remains one of the great pioneers of science. Through a lifetime of devoted study and well-documented research, he took the first steps in separating astronomy from astrology. He was one of the first scientists to theorize that the laws of science do not always coincide with what appears to be true.

Copernicus was much like another man of his age, Columbus, who did not exactly understand what he had discovered but who blazed a trail for fellow explorers. Although Copernicus's heliocentric theory was not widely accepted until long after his death, he was the pioneer who set Kepler, Galileo, and other astronomers on the path toward scientific enlightenment. By doing so, Copernicus helped to remove science from the realm of superstition.

Many scientists who have achieved great fame have changed the way people live. Copernicus's great contribution was not a change in the way people live but in the way they think. Because he allowed people to see the universe differently, he also changed the way scientists were perceived by other people. No longer would they be thought of as fortune-tellers. Instead, they would be regarded as advanced thinkers. In the 1830s, the German scientist and writer Johann von Goethe wrote: "Of all discoveries and opinions, none may have exerted a greater effect on the human spirit than the doctrine of Copernicus. The world had scarcely become known as round and complete in itself when it was asked to waive the tremendous privilege of being the center of the universe."[14]

IMPORTANT DATES

1454	Printing press is developed in Europe.
1473	Mikolaj Kopernik is born in Toruń, Poland.
1483	Kopernik's father dies, his uncle Lucas Waczenrode is named as his guardian.
1491–1495	Copernicus studies at the University of Krakow, Poland.
1492	Columbus lands in North America.
1496	Copernicus begins law studies in Bologna, Italy.
1496–1499	Copernicus studies astronomy under Domenico Maria de Novara.
1497	Copernicus is named to the post of canon at Frombork, Poland. Copernicus and de Novara observe a lunar eclipse.
1500	Copernicus lectures on mathematics in Rome.
1501	Copernicus begins the study of medicine in Padua, Italy, while continuing to read law.
1503	Copernicus is awarded a doctor of canon law degree; he receives a license to practice medicine.
1507	Copernicus becomes the private physician of his uncle, the bishop of Ermeland; he works on his version of the heliocentric theory.
1517	Luther defies the church.
1519	Teutonic Knights attack Polish cities.
1520	Copernicus organizes the defense of the city of Olsztyn against the Teutonic Knights.
1528	Copernicus works on money policy for Duke Albert of Royal Prussia, for whom he serves as an economic adviser.
1539	Georg Rhäticus, professor of mathematics from Wittenberg, Germany, visits Copernicus to learn more about his theory and to assist Copernicus in getting published.

IMPORTANT DATES

1540	*Narratio Prima* is published with a preface by Rhäticus.
1542	*On the Revolution of the Celestial Orbs* is published with a note inserted by Andreas Osiander, a Lutheran cleric whom Rhäticus had recruited to aid in the book's publication.
1543	Copernicus dies.

FOR MORE INFORMATION

BOOKS

Catherine Andronik, *Copernicus: Founder of Modern Astronomy.* Berkeley Heights, NJ: Enslow, 2002. A biography of Copernicus written for readers in middle grades.

Wilbur Applebaum, ed., *Encyclopedia of the Scientific Revolution: From Copernicus to Newton.* New York: Garland, 2000. A reference book of scientific advances made during the Renaissance.

John Henry, *Moving Heaven and Earth: Copernicus and the Solar System.* Melbourne, Australia: Totem Books, 2001. Biography of Copernicus for high school level readers.

WEBSITES

Astronomy Rocks! Nicolaus Copernicus
www.intelligentchild.com
A good biographical site with overview of heliocentric theory.

The Copernican Model: A Sun-Centered Solar System
http://csep10.phys.utk.edu/astr161
A excellent site with shockwave demonstrations of astronomical concepts.

Nicholaus Copernicus Museum in Fromberg
www.frombork.art.pl
A good source of photographs and original manuscripts.

GLOSSARY

armillary sphere: An instrument used to track and measure the movement of celestial bodies.

astrolabe: An instrument used to observe and calculate the position of celestial bodies.

astrology: Determination of the effect of stars and planets on human behavior.

astronomy: Study of objects outside of Earth's atmosphere.

bishop: A clergyman ranked above a priest.

canon: Administrator of a church or diocese.

cardinal: High official of the Catholic Church who ranks below the pope.

eclipse: Total or partial obscuring of one celestial body by another.

epicycle: Circle in which a planet moves while at the same time orbiting a larger celestial body.

geocentric theory: The belief that Earth is the center of the universe.

geometry: Branch of mathematics that measures angles, planes, and surfaces.

heliocentric theory: The belief that the Sun is the center of the solar system.

hypothesis: Assumption made for the sake of argument.

spherical: Having a globular shape.

trigonometry: Branch of mathematics that studies the properties of triangles.

zodiac: Imaginary arc in space divided into twelve constellations.

NOTES

1. Quoted in J.J. O'Connor and E.F. Robertson, "Nicolaus Copernicus," MacTutor History of Mathematics Archive, Turnbull WWW Server. www-gap.dcs.st-and.ac.uk.

2. Quoted in O'Connor and Robertson, "Nicolaus Copernicus."

3. Quoted in O'Connor and Robertson, "Nicolaus Copernicus."

4. Quoted in O'Connor and Robertson, "Nicolaus Copernicus."

5. Quoted in Granville C. Henry, "The Earth-Centered Universe," in *Christianity and the Images of Science* Macon, GA: Smyth and Helwys, 2002. www.helwys.com.

6. Quoted in O'Connor and Robertson, "Nicolaus Copernicus."

7. Quoted in O'Connor and Robertson, "Nicolaus Copernicus."

8. Quoted in *Starry Messenger,* "Ptolemy and Copernicus on Their Cosmological Postulates." www.hps.cam.ac.uk.

9. Quoted in *Starry Messenger,* "Ptolemy and Copernicus on Their Cosmological Postulates."

10. Nicolaus Copernicus, *De Revolutionibus Orbium Coelestium.* Fromberg, Poland: Nicholaus Copernicus Museum in Fromberg, vol. 1, chap. 10. www.frombork.art.pl.

11. Copernicus, *De Revolutionibus,* vol. 1, chap. 10.

12. Quoted in *Starry Messenger,* "Ptolemy and Copernicus on Their Cosmological Postulates."

13. O'Connor and Robertson, "Nicolaus Copernicus."

14. Johann von Goethe, "Goethe's Comment on Copernicus," Dr. Darkwater Presents the Electronic Universe. http://zebu.uoregon.edu.

INDEX